BE THE
WATER

Life Lessons Taught By Nature

Be the Water
By Cheri Henke Kretsch

Publisher's Cataloging-In-Publication Data
(Prepared by The Donohue Group, Inc.)

Names: Kretsch, Cheri Henke, author.
Title: Be the Water / Cheri Henke Kretsch.
Description: [Littleton, Colorado] : [Natural Lessons, LLC], [2018] | Series: Life lessons taught by nature ; book 2
Identifiers: ISBN 9781732913523 | ISBN 9781732913530 (ebook)
Subjects: LCSH: Water--Psychological aspects. | Water--Poetry. | Water--Pictorial works. | Conduct of life. | Adaptability (Psychology) | Respect.
Classification: LCC BF353.5.N37 K742 2018 (print) | LCC BF353.5.N37 (ebook) | DDC 155.91--dc23

Library of Congress Control Number: 2018913244

www.natural-lessons.com

BE THE
WATER

Life Lessons Taught By Nature

CHERI HENKE KRETSCH

Dedication

This is a book about water and the metaphors it brings us about life. It's a constant reminder of the ebb and flow of survival and the connections necessary to create a loving and fulfilled life. Sometimes the connections are in a one-to-one friendship and sometimes they are in a group of friends. All friendships are necessary to make one's life feel valuable and precious. So I'd like to thank the following people for being in my life and making it so rich and fulfilled.

John and Ellie A., Cindy B., Gary B., Nancy B., Shirley B., Nancy C., Drake E., Michael G., Elizabeth H., Debra J., Pam K., Larry R. and Sue M., Sharlyna M., Zoe R., Laura S., Natasha S., Mary K. W., Trisha W.F., Kate W., and Marne W.

A continued "Thank you" for standing beside me, loving me, and encouraging me: to my husband Hunts, my family Cindy, Wayne, Dick, Dee, Wade, and long-time friends Cathy, Pat, Debbie, Ed, and Barbara.

Thank you all for helping to create the person I have evolved to be. Thank you for allowing me into your lives. Thanks for the laughter, joy, and challenges that you've given me. Thank you for being YOU and sharing your precious, gentle, and loving friendships. I deeply cherish you all!

EARTH'S LESSONS

We are all mountains
    strength at its peak
    potential is endless
    challenge we seek.

We are all valleys
    with bruises so deep
    to be at the bottom
    through climbing we weep.

We are all rocks
    secure as a whole
    the pile then crumbles
    new places to go.

We are all grasses
    moving with ease
    a swaying contentment
    it's all such a breeze.

I am with nature
    for as long as I please
    I thank you, Mother Earth,
    for the lessons about me.

CONTENTS

LESSONS FROM WATER

Oh, simple rain
With your sweet smell
Enhancing the senses
Nature beckons to tell.

Oh, simple mist
A soft mystical play
Enhancing spirit
A moment's display.

Oh, simple river
Winding in grasses and trees
Encouraging curiosity
Wonderment in ease.

Oh, simple lake
Depth teaming with life
Expecting discovery
Silence stops the strife.

Oh, simple ocean
Methodical imposing awe
Expanding motion of openness
A magical sunset, I saw.

Oh, connecting water on the earth
In simplicity and might
Elegantly trusting Nature
I know that all is right.

Photo Location: Mille Lac Lake, Brainerd, Minnesota

BE THE WATER

Water is the essence of survival. Without it nothing can exist on this planet. The Earth is about 71 percent water. Our bodies are 55 percent – 65 percent water at any given time. We can only live without it for three to seven days depending upon environmental conditions. So water is what keeps everything living and healthy, flowing, and connected.

Water reminds us of what it means to be alive—to be healthy—and to be mentally and emotionally strong. It helps us physically by lubricating the joints, flushing out toxins and regulating our body temperature, just to name a few. Mentally, water can show us clarity in depth and personal reflection. It helps us to choose the kind of ripple effect we want to exhibit to others. Emotionally, water provides us the opportunity to either stay frozen or see possibilities, to normalize life's journey or stay stuck in its pain, or to decide to fight our way upstream or flow freely downstream.

All in all, water is a part of our lives in every way. If we choose to see, hear, touch, smell, and taste our world we'll understand why the element of water is so important. Listen and observe, and see how nature provides us with answers that are consistent and helpful to our lives. This book is a way to enhance your respect of nature's gift of water. Flow with me through the waterways and learn how to love and respect the element of water on a whole new level. Learn how to honor yourself by honoring nature's finely crafted tools of survival, beauty through appreciation, and strength through understanding.

Let's talk about the human journey, flowing through life, with our teacher, called water.

THE AGGRESSOR

Do not make me
What you want
Or ask me to conform.

Do not beg me
To give up
Or ask me to be torn.

Do not abuse me
My voice dismissed
Or ask me to perform.

Do not control me
I'm not a puppet—
I'm a shining soul.

Do not ask of me
I am not less.
No demands to seize!

Photo Location: Kilauea Lighthouse, Kauai, Hawaii

CHAPTER 1

POWER: AGGRESSIVE OR ASSERTIVE?

POWERFUL WATER: AGGRESSIVE OR ASSERTIVE

While water often brings to mind calm waves, it can also teach us about assertiveness or aggression. I think of assertive water like a swiftly moving river after a downpour. It's motivated with a purpose but not destructive. When I think of an aggressive form of water, I see the tsunami waves slamming into the coastline. The impact gouging out stones and dirt, falling away from the coastline, leaving it changed forever. While both are impactful, one remains normal and the other destructive. Consider the power of the Old Faithful geyser in Yellowstone National Park (it shoots 140 – 190 feet in the air), or a spring run-off swiftly flowing its way into a mighty river. Or a glacier forging out a valley, or a natural spring bubbling to the surface creating a babbling brook. One thing we know for sure is that nature creates change whether it be slow and methodical or through devastating power and force. So first of all, let's look at what happens through aggression, power, and force.

Aggressive people are very much like the aggressive water events. The keyword here is *event*. Whatever is done through power and force always creates an event. Whether it's a spouse fighting, a boss swearing, a teen yelling, or a driver's road rage, it's all creating fear for a purpose. If you're the recipient or victim, it is an event that you'll not soon forget. Nature shows us that aggressiveness almost always has long-term effects. She changes the river's path after a flood, rocks erode at a seashore from crashing waves, or trees and bushes are shredded after a severe hailstorm. It is no different than the fight that leads to divorce, the boss who gets fired for harassment, the teen being grounded for disrespect, or the driver going to jail for road rage.

Aggressiveness means hostile or violent behavior, determined and forceful. An aggressive stance from either nature or mankind means, "Watch-out, nothing good is going to happen here." Forceful people are usually *controlling* people. They want their world to be what they want and compromising is not an option. It's like that old adage, "It's my way or the highway." The typical forceful person is both fearful and insecure. They need to control everything around them or their world will fall apart and their needs won't get met. It's actually a very sad place to be. Fear rules their heart and mind. Nonetheless, their behavior needs to change and if they won't do it proactively then consequences will teach them after the fact. Their behavior is their issue: they belittle, discount, demean, embarrass, make you cower in fear, or leave you thinking that there is nothing that they won't do to you to destroy your life. Anyone who can create that in another human being has a problem. In all likelihood, you didn't cause or create the problem or event. The origins of this event were already on their destructive path long before you came along. But there are lessons for everyone in these scenarios. As a recipient you're probably going to learn how not to take things personally, how to stand up for yourself, and how to communicate with difficult people. Most importantly, you have to learn how to take care of *you*. Do whatever is necessary to take proper care of you and not become a victim or a contributor to the bully mentality. It's not up to you to lessen *their* consequences, let them fall where they may. Take a stand (if you can), report to a person of authority, leave, always be around them with someone else present (don't be alone with them), don't fall for the apologies or gifts if it's already happened once before. Communication should never make someone else feel bad, ashamed, or fearful. Communication should be about listening, respect, and active problem solving to make things work better in the future. Assertiveness skills help us to do just that.

With so many years of listening to situations regarding an aggressive person, I do believe that assertiveness is a better way. The consequences of the aggressor can be so damaging to all people involved. In nature, and with people, assertiveness is about being confident but respectful. In nature we see a milder form of *get ready* as the river swells, giving warning of weak spots on the river banks. The smaller tidal waves give caution of what could happen if they were from a larger tsunami, and the gentle snow falls to let us know what we might need in order to be prepared in case of a blizzard. For people, the *get ready* warning looks like sitting down with a person in conflict and sharing your points of view while being open enough to hear the other side. It's being able to tell someone that your feelings have been hurt and allowing them to express remorse, or explain themselves. It's taking a leadership role, yet allowing others an opportunity to grow. Assertiveness is not coming in and directing, overpowering, or demeaning others to get things done. It is about being open, allowing growth for all involved, sharing one's truth or beliefs without being superior, or making suggestions, but not having to win over everyone to your side. Here are a few tips to becoming more assertive:

1. Decide that you want to positively assert yourself.

2. Aim for a respectful and honest discussion—keep your head in the right place even if the other person can't.

3. Learn to listen and listen to learn.

4. Ask questions to clarify and find out where they're coming from.

5. Avoid guilt trips and bringing up past events, conflicts—stay in the future as much as possible. Example: What can we do to make this work out better for both of us in the future?

6. Stay in your head, NOT your emotions—stay calm.

7. Look to problem-solve the situation. Example: How do you see this _____ working out? How could I be more helpful in the future?

8. If the aggressive person won't have a decent conversation, then say something like: "I'll be glad to talk to you when we can have a conversation that is beneficial to both you and me." Then leave. If you haven't heard from them in a couple of days you may want to call and see if you can arrange a time to have a problem-solving discussion.

9. No matter how this goes, it is your human right to be treated respectfully. Act as if you should have that respect. Then, treat others as you want to be treated.

Assertiveness is about letting people know where you stand without having to put someone else down. Assertiveness is about good people learning to communicate at a level of self-respect and self-empowerment—then sharing those skills with others.

Be the Water
Know you deserve to be treated respectfully, then treat others the same. Be Assertive.

INSIGHTS TO PONDER

1. So who gets your *feisty* going? What is it about them that feeds that angst in you?

2. Are there events or topics that really get you going, bringing out these feelings more often than not?
   - Do comments make you feel inadequate, embarrassed, or ashamed?
   - Do you feel disrespected, humiliated, or not heard?
   - Do events trigger you? One-on-one vs. larger group, being the expert vs. being told what to do by others? Are you tired, stressed, depressed, or overanxious?
   - Do you see your response to others as aggressive or assertive?
   - How do others see you? Aggressive or Assertive? What responses tell you so?

3. How are others responding to you? Are they fearful, overly compliant, or sheepish? Do they want to talk with you? Do they feel that you'll listen? Can you agree to disagree and still find a way to manage this better in the future?

4. Do you have someone who talks down to you? How would you like to respond or act? (Knowing the goal is respectful, honest, and concerned.)

5. How do you see yourself in dealing with conflict? How would you rate your effectiveness with difficult people? Use the scale 1 (low success) to 10 (generally great success). What might you do to better your success score?

Make a plan for how to deal with difficult people. Research several ways and find one that you're willing to try. Visualize it several times. Redo past scenarios—see yourself successful.

LEARNING IS SURVIVAL

To Learn
    is the freedom to accomplish
    to feel something great
    to be something new.

No Man
    is whole if he stops learning
    he just starts taking
    just stops living.

There will always be
    a new hand to touch
    a new feeling to feel
    a new place to explore.

Life is uncertain
    Learning is captivating
    Learning is necessary
    Learning is survival.

CHAPTER 2

ALL LESSONS ARE IMPORTANT

WATERFALLS SHOW US THAT ALL LESSONS ARE IMPORTANT

Waterfalls—the beauty, the roar, the gentleness. Their free-flowing water tumbling down, down, down, into a pool at the bottom. What I find so fascinating about waterfalls is that no matter how far the water falls or how wide or narrow it starts, or the power it creates, it all ends in the pool at the bottom and then continues on its way. Looking at life, I see it very much the same way: no matter how open or narrow we think, no matter how far we tumble and fall, we get to the bottom and then continue on. Nature is so amazing in how she shows us that life, no matter what happens, will continue.

At one point in my life, I would have said that the height of the fall determines who suffers the most—whose life should be considered more painful than someone else's. That the person who was hit by the two-by-four had it harder than the person who just got a slap on the hand. It seemed that some people suffer through one difficulty after another while others just get a bump on the road. But what I've learned is that all difficulties are lessons. It's about the emotion tied to it, not the event itself. Loss is loss. If a child loses his pet turtle in death it is just as devastating at that moment as the death of a family member later on in life. The child's tears are no less sad than the tears of an adult. Another example would be in love: Is that high school relationship any less important than the long-term marriage? Have you known someone who after a marriage ended through death or divorce, reconnected with a childhood sweetheart? The deep connection of the emotional love created by the childhood sweetheart is no less than a long-term marriage. Different, yes, but both emotionally impactful. We really don't have the right to say that one event is more or less impactful than another based on age, event, or emotion. Two people could have a similar event happen in their lives yet each responds differently to its sense of difficulty. One could be devastated and another only momentarily set back. However the person interprets the difficulty is how the impact will be determined.

One factor in determining how we see and feel an event is through the skills we've already acquired. With each success of 'getting through' we internally praise ourselves for figuring out the solution and moving on. As we build on those successes, we become confident in our ability to handle the next ones.

The second factor is memory. When a situation arises our brain automatically searches our memory banks to see if something similar has happened in the past. That information then gives us the direction to problem-solve the current issue facing us. Usually, the issue becomes more pronounced until we really work through it. Sometimes we look back and don't have the satisfaction that it went well or was completed. If you don't want the same reaction from your past, then here's a way to help retrain your brain before the next similar event happens again:

1. Go back into the memory of a troubling event.

2. Pull it up and bring as many details to the forefront as possible. Be the observer. Watch yourself as you relive that memory. What do you wish you'd done differently?

3. Re-envision the memory to look the way you'd like it to. Re-program your brain to picture how you want to act in the future. Do this several times until it feels more natural to react the way you want.

4. When a similar event occurs in the future, your brain will bring up the original and the reimagined memories for you to work with. The *feeling* of the memory will solidify the new version. So feel it as deeply and as often as you can. Feel its success, regardless of how the other person may react. If you're a visual person—visualize (see) yourself in your new memory as actually accomplishing the task or getting through the event. Do it at least ten times. See if you feel more confident as you take on another difficulty.

A third factor is transferred learning. When I taught handicapped high school students, I learned a lot about the many ways our brains work and the ability to learn. I learned to be appreciative and have gratitude for what a healthy brain is capable of doing. Transferred learning was fascinating to me. I had one young man who I was training to cross the street, looking both ways before crossing. He was able to correctly cross the street on which we practiced, but a different street was like a brand new concept to him. His brain wouldn't transfer what he learned to do at one street to do it on all streets.

Think about how much you learn through your brain's ability to transfer information and find relatedness. We do this physically, mentally, emotionally, and spiritually. Transferred learning is a huge factor in how we build our abilities to deal with new situations. Appreciate the fact that your brain is geared toward transferring information that has the slightest similarity. You see, it doesn't matter how far the waterfall falls, what matters is the journey it is on. The waterfall tumbles—we tumble. The waterfall falls into a pool—we gather our resources, of all kinds, and re-establish ourselves. The water from the waterfall continues on its path, be it into a stream, river, lake, or ocean—we, too, continue on our journeys.

So a lesson is a lesson. If someone has a hard lesson, they're better equipped with the abilities to handle the next level of difficulties. They may learn something new or something deeper about themselves. They may learn a new resource, or to change the perspective, but there is always something to be learned. We need to stop comparing ourselves to others. We catch ourselves saying, "They must be more together because they got through it faster," or, "I could never have gotten through that," or, "I should have known that." Our life experiences are unique just like waterfalls, teaching us that there is beauty in the fall. We, too, are beautiful beings no matter what we've been through. Everyone gets bruised up on their journey. So let's not measure our worth or another person's worth based on the amount of tragedies or difficulties they've had. Every waterfall in your life is meant to be a challenge to you. If you knew how to do everything, life would be exceptionally boring. Accept your challenges to see whom you might become. Honor your path and honor the paths of others.

Be the Waterfall
Value ALL Lessons Learned

INSIGHTS TO PONDER

1. Take a look at your waterfalls—your difficulties. How have you endured?
   - How did you get through it or around it?
   - How did you know what to do or try?
   - What abilities did you use to overcome these difficulties?

2. Is there a theme in how you overcome difficulties? Write down several situations that were difficult. How did you get through them? A thought, a saying, a person, etc.? Do you have confidence in this ability to help you again?

3. While your waterfalls were presenting themselves, what good things were happening at the same time?
   - What kept you going forward?
   - What was your hope in getting through?
   - Looking back, would you have done it differently? If so, what do you wish you'd have done?
   - Using that re-imagining technique, how could it have turned out?

4. List five positive character/personality traits that have become stronger or deeper because of difficulties.

5. Looking into the future how do you choose to look at difficulties:
   - They hurt me and leave me wounded—I hope I don't get anymore!
   - They are what they are—I'll get through
   - I know I will grow with each difficulty—bring it on.

A MEMORY

I had a memory
it started to fade away.
No, no I need that memory
I'm begging you to stay
    Searching
    Seeking
    Knowing——   I needed it
                         I loved it

I went into a world
that kept me in a bind
Oh, how I cried
That memory—I sighed

I can't keep it
I shouldn't keep it
    Listen
    Think
    Feel——   Did I want it?
                   Did I need it?

I had a memory
Yet moving on without it
Oh, memory, I beg
Release me from your grip.

CHAPTER 3

FROZEN IN TIME

CRYSTALLIZED WATER – FROZEN IN TIME

Crystallized water—ice! I just can't help thinking of the animated movie *Frozen*. It reminds me how ice was a curse, something to fear, and yet it produced a magical beauty. How often in life have we felt stuck or *frozen* and yet in the end we learned so much more about ourselves, our *beauty*?

Ice is a temporary situation. Even glaciers, thick and seemingly solid, are moving and changing constantly. As nature thaws out her ice she exposes more of herself. We see streams, flowers, and rocks. We're much like the ice. When an issue has occurred we often deal with it as best we can at the time. But more often than not, it's been emotionally packed away deep within the archives of the brain. It's become *frozen* in time. But frozen in thought and frozen in emotions are two distinctly different things.

Unfortunately, we've often come to the conclusion that if we had dealt with the issue *properly*, right up front, we shouldn't have to deal with it again. Once we've worked it through, we feel as though we should be done with it. We believe that a difficulty should be a short-term deal. But thinking it does not remove or make it so. As our brain and emotions mature we have the capability to understand that concern at a deeper level. Often, the really difficult issues of our past will be revisited in the future but with a maturing of the thoughts and feelings.

Not only do we try to think things through, but we also know there are feelings attached and a physical/biological effect. These are the factors that get triggered, as they morph into a tangled spider's web. The brain takes anything "relatable" to the core issue, then builds and packs on more and more events, making it thick and difficult to get to. Think about the frozen river, the ice gets thicker and thicker holding the weight of a man or a car, until spring when it can finally begin to thaw. How does the brain morph a difficulty into something so deep that it's hard to find its core source? For example: let's say you were a victim of a car accident going through an intersection. First you'll want to avoid that same intersection for a while (fear). Months down the road, you may find yourself always going to a lighted intersection—it just gives you a little more safety. Then, as time goes on, you now only merge onto freeways where there will be an extended merging lane—or not go on a freeway at all, less chance of an accident.

See where I'm going with this? Our brain is made to keep us safe—protect us. It sends us signals to watch out for similar situations. But the brain is also creative. It will start protecting you in ways that might be remotely linked. If our driving example would have continued, this person would become fearful of driving all together. The creative brain would have broadened the fear to the unpredictability of people. Through that creative expansion, now the fear-based driver may only consider going to social events where they know all the people. They won't have to worry about others being unpredictable.

Your brain can take one fear and expand it to many different avenues, all needing to be protected. It goes where it wants to—often without your awareness or permission to do so. When transferred learning occurs, it can be a benefit to us, such as making the leap from crossing one street to any street, or it can harm you, such as transferring fearful information which produces an overprotective brain. The brain is so sly you won't even notice it until one day you realize your life is being minimized or manipulated by fear. You've become so overprotective that life isn't enjoyable or fun. You've become *frozen* in fear.

The thawing out process begins when you can see what is holding you hostage through the unconscious. The hard part is that it's often difficult to find the core of the spider web from which the concern arose in the first place. So the web's layers have become thick over time. In other words, so much time has passed that the layers of processed fears have grown so thick it's now difficult to get to the core of the initial problem. In therapy, we often refer to getting to the core issue as 'peeling an onion' one layer at a time—it's just like a slow-moving glacier: one small piece at a time will thaw out and move it along. Sometimes the brain is so ready to be done with the over-protection that it allows a large section to give way. That frozen feeling is now being exposed. It is ready to deal with a larger piece from the frozen/fearful past event.

There is no right or wrong way for the brain to deal with these past issues. If it has spent a lot of time protecting you—it's not going to allow too much vulnerability to occur. If the wisdom or development of the brain is at a new level of under-standing of the issue, the brain may allow a larger piece to be exposed, knowing you are capable of handling it. With the exception of mental illness, our brain knows what is in our best interest. Learning is extremely powerful. Our thoughts can start opening the door to understanding. Through thought the brain says "You get it now and are capable of feeling it."

Most often we can use our intelligent thoughts to understand what happened. However, our emotions are much deeper and usually require assistance to really deal with their impact. You will never relive the intense feelings from the initial event because you've processed it through your thoughts (which is a survival tool—thank heavens!), but the feelings attached to the event are more difficult to understand. Emotions are how we feel wounded and vulnerable. We all have that little child in us that needs a hug or a Band-Aid to make our world feel a little bit safer and compassionate. We need to be heard when we've been hurt or wronged. So listen to that small inner voice and soothe it, honor it, or talk to someone who can listen with empathy. In a short time you'll be ready to take on the world once again.

An event, whether you believe it was traumatic or not, is up to the brain and the heart (emotions) to make the call to stay conscious or go unconscious. So often, when I used a trauma technique called Eye Movement Desensitization Reprocessing (EMDR), the client was surprised to find what was at the core of the issue. At this time in their lives they thought it was no big deal or just plain silly, but their brains at the time of the event didn't think so. The brain chose to store that bruise away into the subconscious. That bruise could have been a word, a gesture, feelings of embarrassment, shame, feelings of inadequacies, as well as the big ones of abuse, death, and violence. Your brain calculated that process for many events throughout your life. Consequently, it built up over time. One day you find yourself saying, "Why am I so sad—I don't have any reason to be so?" or "Why am I so angry every time something little happens?" At that time, the senses are in maximum utilization giving our brain information to sort out. That's why people will remember things they touched, what it tasted like, how something smelled, what they saw, or what they heard. Each event is interpreted through all the senses, then sent to the brain to figure out how to deal with it.

Shock is often a part of an event. If the brain can't make sense of the information it's received it puts the emotions on 'hold' (shock). It feels like your body is numb. You're going through the motions but you can't put feelings to it, "I know I should cry . . . but I can't." Shock can last for minutes, weeks, or months. Then the brain will tuck away the memory of the event until it gets enough information to make sense out of it. If it's too much impact (psychologically, emotionally, and/or physically) at the time the event occurred, we often see people who now have Post Traumatic Stress Disorder (PTSD). PTSD is the spiderweb based in fear of the unexplainable, deep inside the unconscious mind. It can be very complex—no one should underestimate its seriousness. There are so many different types, severities, and explanations, that research is just now starting to help us understand its complexities. I have over-simplified this diagnosis for a basic understanding here. PTSD is the brain's way of protecting the human body—it is physical survival. After the initial shock, the brain will categorize the memory into a snippet of an event or a part of the event. That's why PTSD looks different for each person. Some may go on with a normal life for many years, then seemingly, out of the blue, the brain says, "It's time!" They now find themselves being irritated or sad within when triggered by subject matter close to their memories. It just took the brain time to mature into the understanding of the past. Some people will seek out treatments right after an event happened and try to learn to handle it. Some get symptoms to remind them that the brain is trying to deal with it such as nightmares, a startling effect from noises, or headaches. Some have no symptoms for many years, then one day they are in full blown PTSD.

No matter how the brain chooses to deal with the situation, the goal is to try to make sense out of it. It's not about making it right or wrong, it's about finding a place of peace where we can live with what has been handed to us. Learn to accept that your brain has a unique way of helping you through difficult times that are hard to understand. Accept that you may not immediately know what to do with those hardships. You do the best you can with the information you have at the time. Your brain takes over and helps you to survive using any tool it can. Accept that your brain has learned to protect you from falling apart for the rest of your life.

We, as adults, often look back and question, "Why did I react that way?" or "Why did I decide to be super responsible?" "Why did I become super shy, or super aggressive toward authority?" We want to beat up that innocent child within us for not knowing what to do, wishing he/she would have made a better decision. Totally unfair! Maybe that child learned to be quiet in harsh times, or to put on a mask of "everything is alright," or to become a class clown, or a perfectionist. Whatever the brain chose to do in those moments, it did so to the preservation of *you*. Respect what was chosen, don't beat it up as inadequate. Realize that no adult, much less a child, should have been put into such a fearful event. Their brains should never have been in the position to make those survival decisions. Use your wisdom, don't be judgmental of yourself or others. Know that many things happen to us, and that your brain is working toward your betterment—even if it's at a subconscious level.

So just as Nature knows how to thaw out a river of ice or send a glacier to cut out a valley, she knows it's all about timing and allowing the ice to thaw as needed. Our brains have given us the ability of timing and allowing us to gather what we need to keep us moving along in our lives. Know there is nothing wrong with you as you mature and relive difficult issues—it's normal. It's just your brain saying you're ready to understand it at a newly acquired mature level.

Be the Crystallized Water
Know there is no set time for the unconscious to rise from its frozen state—when it happens, it is the right time. You now have the ability to work through it successfully.

INSIGHTS TO PONDER

1. What difficult events have you experienced? Write them down.

2. Looking at that list, how do you feel? Look at each one separately—how do you feel about each one?

3. As you look at each event, what do you notice through your senses? Is there a particular thing you see, hear, smell, taste, or touch?

4. Did your fear from that event transfer into other situations ('spiderweb')?

5. How did you deal with the situation back then? How are you judging it now?

6. What coping skill did you learn to help you get through it? Do you still use it today? If not, what new skill replaced it?

7. Have you ever been in shock? What did it feel like? What did you notice about it? Did you react while in shock? How did that look?

8. Do you honor your brain for giving you time and space to slowly figure out what happened and how you got through the event/difficulty? Do you see the difference in your maturity level now versus back then? How do you honor the capacity of your brain to protect and help you?

9. Are the coping skills you developed from a past event still appropriate today? Do you need to discard them? What new skill would you replace it with?

LETTING GO OF HARDSHIPS

It's scary
to let go
of all
I've ever
known.

Its history
brings me tears
Yet in wisdom
how I've
grown.

Photo Location: Kebler Pass, Crested Butte, Colorado.

CHAPTER 4

OBSTACLES

WATER AND OBSTACLES

I always love looking at the river. I see huge boulders, simple stones, fallen trees, or debris throughout the river's path. It reminds me of how life really is. In the river there are huge boulders that can seemingly alter or almost stop the water from flowing down its path. We can have large boulders in our lives, too. They're the things we have no control over—like death, abuse, divorce, accidents, physical impairments, etc. They can be so devastating that we almost stop living. It's hard to find rhyme or reason to move forward. Yet, like the river, some part of us does keep going.

Then there are the stepping stones that help us get to the other side without stopping the flow of water, instead just creating small diversions from a flawless journey. Rivers are never on a perfectly straight journey. They have many twists and turns. Rivers create beauty through their journey. We, too, get stepping stones or diversions from our life's paths. We meet new people, are presented with an opportunity, move to a new state, receive a promotion, or rescue a pet. With each new thing that happens, we stop our path, contemplate our journey, and decide what to do next. There can be positive diversions or discouraging diversions, but nothing that will stop us from moving on. They simply challenge us.

Looking at the dead trees or debris floating down the river, I notice that they eventually get stuck along the river's path. Sometimes they're stuck for a moment, maybe longer, but the water works through it and continues on its way. Only when a lot of debris has gathered in one spot do we notice it taking its toll on the river. How often do we get stuck in our past, in a situation or a place where we don't want to be? Maybe we're stuck in a job, in a financial situation, having a health problem, having to move away from a home or place that we don't want to leave, or involved in a challenging relationship. Yet, with time and help, we keep on flowing onward on our life's journey.

I've never seen a river without obstacles. Nor have I ever seen a person without issues, difficulties, or hard times. What we learn from a river is to keep on flowing, no matter what. That there is no obstacle big enough, except death itself, to stop us from continuing on our path of life. We should expect a huge boulder in our path at some point, as well as the stepping stone opportunities, and the debris we've collected to deal with along the way.

Sometimes we forget that these obstacles are what made our lives *normal*. If too much debris has gathered, then it may be time to declutter your life and deal with whatever is building up. Is a past fear slowing you down because you're being too overprotective, too perfect, too cautious? When your life feels like it's closing in instead of opening up to newness and change, then maybe look for the debris and see if you can't release yourself from the build-up. Sometimes a friend, a family member, a therapist, a boss, a minister or a teacher could be helpful in sharing something that they notice but that you may not see. Being open to someone else's ideas, thoughts, or feelings may be all you need to start flowing/moving once again. If you have big boulders in your path, look at how you can break them up into smaller pieces to deal with one small piece at a time. Just as nature sends the flood to clear away the obstacles, so too do we have to find a way to clear out the debris. It's okay to take some introspection time and look at the obstacles you're facing. Then make a plan, and act on it. When you clear your heart and mind you'll see new opportunities—new ways of thinking and feeling. Go for it!!

Be the Water
Declutter or break down the obstacles
that keep holding you back.

INSIGHTS TO PONDER

1. Just like the river, we face obstacles. Sometimes the obstacles stop us from doing something that would be better for us. Can you remember a time when fear was becoming out of hand and trying to stop you in your tracks?
   - What was going on? What made you notice?
   - What coping skill did you use to get through it?
   - Where did that coping skill come from?

2. How do you handle your accumulated debris?
   - List the past difficulties that you have accumulated—physically, emotionally, and mentally.
   - Have you already challenged some of that debris? Which ones?
   - If one of these fears has 'spiderwebbed' into something much greater, what would your next step be to master this fear?
   - Can you see how much you've already grown through the fears?
   - How has it been a benefit to you by taking these steps to master your fears?
   - List how you've grown, developed coping skills, and how you problem-solve your difficulties.
   - Look into your future. Did you master some of your fears? What did life look like?
   - What thoughts, mottos, or sayings help you to continue on your life's journey?

CHAOS

Sometimes
I feel
up or down
going straight
or
all around.

Sometimes
I feel
here or there
feeling the pains
that lead
no-where.

Sometimes
I feel
a calming peace
chaos subdued
I sense
my release.

CHAPTER 5

EXTERNAL CHURNING, INTERNAL CALM

THE WATER IS CHURNING YET CALM

As I look out over a lake or an ocean, I can't help but ponder the difference between the surface and the depth. There can be crashing waves on the surface yet a peaceful calm the deeper you go. One body of water and such a dichotomy. I sense that the surface of an ocean is like the external world of how we see ourselves and others. It's the world of goals and dreams with judgment and expectations. It is the world of how we see ourselves every day, doing everyday stuff, and blending within our environment. The depth of an ocean or lake is the internal self. It is the intuition, the voice you hear in your head, or the compassion you feel in your heart. It is your internal world of self-knowledge, self-awareness, and self-accountability. Just like the dichotomy of the ocean, we, too, are a dichotomy. How we function or relate in our outside world can look very different from the feelings of our inside world.

Let's look at the whales of the ocean and the monks of a monastery. Bear with me here as I explain. Living in the ocean, whales generally stay in the deeper calm water below the surface. They can choose to come up to the surface for different reasons but the majority of their life is spent in the calm depth of the ocean. Monks, on their quest toward enlightenment, live in a secluded environment learning lessons of internal peace. They, too, can go out into the public occasionally but the majority of their time is spent in the quiet calm of the monastery. Both the whale and the monk know about the churning of the external/surface world, yet they chose to find the calm. The oceans and lakes remind us that no matter how chaotic our lives may seem on the surface we, too, can go deeper and find peaceful contentment, just like the whales and monks.

I continually hear from frustrated people how chaotic our world is. "What are we supposed to do with this mess?" "It's so huge—I feel heavy and upset all the time!" I say, "Look at the whales of the oceans and the monks of the monastery." The whales have learned instinctively how to avoid the surface of the ocean in the middle of a storm. There is just no reason to stay in the thrashing waves when you can take a breath and go back down to the calm. Monks live in monasteries because there is less conflict and chaos while they're learning. It is a place of calm silence. They have to learn to maintain the calmness deep inside themselves. In fact, one of the final tests for a monk is to leave the monastery, stand for hours in a peaceful stance, and let people do what they will to them (no bodily harm), and maintain the peace inside themselves. People have spit on them, cursed just inches from their faces, made fun of them, and so on. Yet they have learned to maintain their sense of peace deep within their soul. I don't know about you, but I know that if I could do that on just a small level, my life would be happier.

The good news is that we can find a peaceful calm inside ourselves. It's a simple concept—but a difficult practice. Even those who find a confidence and purpose to their lives may occasionally be jolted from their sense of contentment. Here are some thoughts to help get us into that place of calm.

- Detach. Your outcome and somebody else's do not have to be the same. Detach your thoughts and judgments toward others and how they live their lives or make their decisions—it's not your business. Their journey is not your journey. Their pain is not your pain, nor is it helpful to determine whose is more painful. Their joy is not your joy, it is the benefit of their own decisions. We are not here to take away any part of someone else's experience. We can educate or inform, that's all we get. Each person will need to take their benefits and hits from life based on their own decisions.

- No roles, no expectations. We need to stop putting people in roles and then judging them based on that. For example: a family connection does not mean you will be best friends or that they'll come running to help you if you need it. Each person is here for their own reason. We are all busy trying to figure out what our purpose is. Just because you share genetics does not mean that you or they will be obligated to be best friends forever. It is still based in respect and choosing to have that person in your life or not. If we lose the roles of what a spouse/partner, boss, or friend should be, we open the door for discovery, curiosity, and awe of what another human being is capable of. We allow each person in the relationship to define the connection. We know that there are bad/difficult people on this planet. Your job is to not get sucked into their negative energy at the cost of your positive energy. If you feel anger, frustration, resentment, or tension, pay attention! It's the opportunity for you to take a step back, go into the 'caution zone', and re-evaluate what's going on. If you feel negative/badly the majority of the time, you'll have to change the relationship's dynamics—take a stand, and talk about your true feelings with them. If this relationship cannot evolve then you'll have to leave. You are here to protect the goodness of *you*. Work at making a better you and better relationships.

- Believe in the goodness of yourself *and* in others. If we get too caught up in what we want, or what others need, we get off track. If we do our best to be good to ourselves *and* others, we develop respect, equality, and honor. If I have a knowledge, skill or talent, I should want to use it to better my life and somehow enrich the lives of others. If we do this, it stops us from spending too much time stuck in self-centeredness, or in believing everyone is more important than you. Stay away from either extreme as entrenchment can only cause you harm. Remember the *'and'* to help keep your life in balance.

- Understand perception. Everyone will see issues, events, relationships, or opportunities differently based on their personality, history, and beliefs. Don't assume that everyone should think or see things as you do. Ask questions to find out what they believe and why. This will alleviate a lot of stress for you. If you can learn to be okay with others' perceptions and their right to see things as they do, whether or not you agree, it will save you needless anxiety, worry, and frustration. Be kind to yourself.

As an individual, we can stay at the surface and fight in the chaotic world or we can learn to be okay with going into the deeper water for peace and calm. We all have so many ways available to us to create what it is we want. I can choose to see only the difficult or I can choose to see the good. I can see the ugly or the beauty. I can choose to be in an abusive relationship or value myself enough to leave it. I can choose to see myself as more than, less than, equal to, or greater than. I get to choose whether I want peace and calm or whether I want to be part of the chaos of the world. Remember that today's situations are temporary. We may choose calm when we're really stressing out or we may choose an activity to help get us motivated. I no longer am stuck in the churning surface water when I've gone into a deeper belief that all people are here at the right time, right place, doing their right thing through the synchronicity of the universe. I have then detached my ego, giving everyone else the right to live their lives however they choose. My only job is to empower, encourage, and love. Sometimes this may mean doing so from a distance. In this busy hectic world, if you want to be the whale or the monk—you can. Know that you're in control.

Be the Water
You can be the external churning or practice the internal calm.

INSIGHTS TO PONDER

1. Rate from 1 (low) to 10 (high) how chaotic your life feels currently.

2. What do you think are the causes of the chaos? List them.

3. Look at your chaos/external world in general:
   - Are there themes in your past that you keep repeating? Are they good for you now?
   - Are there roles that you keep holding onto that define you? Are they good for you now?

4. What do you do when life gets too hectic or crazy? Do you run away and hide, shutting everyone out? Do you get angry and yell when enough is enough? Do you keep on going until something physical takes you down? Do you become a martyr, thinking you must do everything, because no one else can do it right?

5. Look at yourself—how do you explain your chaos? Who's in control?

6. What can you do to create less chaos and have more calm? What can you do to make things more workable? From your list above, write down one step (for each one) you can take to make it more workable.

7. How are you judging yourself or others? Do you see yourself as more than they are or less than they are? How do you detach and still maintain healthy relationships?

8. What are your expectations for yourself or others—by what or whose standard? What roles give you comfort/discomfort? How do you honor each person's right (including yourself) to learn, be, feel, and perceive?

9. How are you balancing the needs of yourself and the needs of others? How do you perceive your life vs. their life? How do you honor both?

NOTES

A NEW DIRECTION

I yearn for the place
to rest my head
A place of contentment
no anger or dread.

I yearn for the mountains
so peaceful and bold
Wildflowers a blooming
so gently unfold.

I yearn for the pasture
so alive and so free
No reason to fear
for miles you can see.

I yearn for the river
so swift, so flowing
The struggle is gone
a relaxed unknowing.

I yearn for a place
to quiet my heart
Take confusion away
accept a new start.

CHAPTER 6

UPSTREAM OR DOWNSTREAM

GOING WITH THE FLOW

How many times have you heard the saying, 'just go with the flow'? Generally this applies to being 'laid back' or just cruising along in life. But for me, it teaches about our choices of going upstream or downstream. On a river, going downstream means you're flowing *with* the current. There's generally minimal physical exertion and you progress easily. If, instead, you decide to go upstream, you're going *against* the flow and everything is much more difficult. You are fighting the current every step of the way, and the movement is slow at best.

The one thing I've noticed about rivers is that they all have rapids and moments of a swift calm. It seems to me that whatever was happening upstream was also happening somewhere downstream. So here's my question. Why would I struggle pushing myself upstream against the current if I'm most likely to encounter a similar experience somewhere downstream when flowing with the current? We often seem to push ourselves against the currents of life, and then get upset that it's so hard. If it's that hard, turn the canoe around and flow downstream. Going upstream is more about being in control than being wise. Look at your past—how many times did you work extra hard, push yourself, or sacrifice your time because you knew it would pay off in the end. At what cost? A divorce, children who don't know you, or someone else getting the promotion or the raise? I'm not saying you shouldn't be motivated, just be so when life's generally flowing downstream. It's a calm feeling when things are running smooth. We just need to recognize that point in the river when you should turn around.

When life is flowing with ease, then you know you're flowing on the right path. If you have one thing after another going against you, you're most likely going against the current, battling upstream. We have to understand that other people are making decisions at the same time that you are. The boss may already know who he/she wants for the new position and no matter how hard you try, you will not change that decision. You may have just gone out with a new love interest thinking all went great, yet he/she doesn't go out with you again. There are many things at work in these situations besides what you believe about any scenario. You do, however, get to choose how you want to react or change course. If you're working hard and have roadblock after roadblock, setback after setback, or battle after battle, it's time to step back and re-evaluate the difficulties with the progress. Maybe it's not the right time, or the right people, or the right place, or maybe you just need more information or education to make a better decision for yourself. So if you're feeling consistently heavy, resentful, burdened, frustrated, or feeling that things are unfair, it's time to turn the canoe around.

Thank heavens that there are always new opportunities, new ways to see situations, or new ways to feel when you change your thoughts. Allow yourself permission to think and feel outside the box you're in. What would you do if you left this stressful job? Where could you live to enjoy your environment more? What would life be like without this relationship—could you find your own way? The good thing about going downstream is that you'll get an opportunity comparable to what you've just experienced but this time things can fall into place—new time, new people, or a new situation. This time things won't be so difficult as long as you are open and willing for the new adventure. But make sure you don't carry the burden of the last job, or the lost partner, or how others treated you, into your new situation. Allow the situation to define itself through your new growth and understanding.

Forcing things to happen rarely works out to your advantage in the long run. Someone might hold a grudge and make you pay for it in the future, or, as they say, karma will get you if you've stepped on others to get where you're going. If it's not good for you—it's probably not good for others either and something will change in the future. So the next time someone says, "Go with the flow," re-evaluate your position in the river. Are you forcing yourself or others to go upstream fighting against the current? Or are you allowing yourself to be open to flowing downstream and seeing what new opportunities await you!

Be the River
Go with the flow—flow with the downstream current of life.

INSIGHTS TO PONDER

1. Think back into your past, and find some memories that took you upstream.
   - What do you notice about the difficulty of it?
   - Did you turn it around and make it easier on yourself? What did you do?
   - Evaluate your energy level. Was it more positive or negative? Did it build you up or wear you down?
   - Thinking of those memories, re-imagine them. What kept you there longer than you needed to be? Where do you wish you would have turned your canoe around? How would your life be different today?

2. Now think of a memory where you chose to flow downstream with a decision you made.
   - How did it feel?
   - How was it on your physical energy?
   - What made you decide to flow with the current rather than fight it?

3. Let's say 80 percent of the time you flow pretty well.
   - What do you tolerate that you should reconsider? Why?
   - What beliefs/decisions do you make that keeps the 80 percent working so well for you?

4. Looking ahead into the future, how do you anticipate 'going with the flow?'

- How would you hope to feel after a difficulty is over?
- How many difficulties will you tolerate until you re-evaluate? (It's helpful to use a current situation).
- What might be the tipping point that makes you turn your canoe around to flow downstream with the current?

NOTES

I WONDER—DO YOU?

Can a leaf feel

       or am I a fool?

When it turns colors

       again is it new?

Can a stick talk

       or am I weird?

When it gets stepped on

       does it cry in fear?

Can the sky be crying

       or am I strange?

When the dark clouds rumble

       and begin to rain?

Do flowers know

       what it's like to die?

Can birds in flight

       wonder why?

Do long heavy snakes

       wish they had legs?

Can a courageous lion

       ever beg?

       Well, perhaps I'm just absurd!

CHAPTER 7

LIGHTNESS AND LAUGHTER

LIGHTNESS AND LAUGHTER

If you've ever been hiking and run across a babbling brook or natural spring, you'll know what I mean when I say, "It just makes you happy." A babbling brook makes a bubbly, gurgling sound. It sounds playful. You can't help but laugh. It's just so, so, bubbly! Though I don't know their origin in every setting, it seems that quite often they come from a natural spring. How cool is that? A little spring bubbling up from the earth just to make us laugh! That little babbling brook reminds me that we need to laugh more, feel lighter, and remember that we, too, have an essence of the playful child within us.

Sometimes our lives get too hectic and out of sorts. We forget to see the laughable or find the sweet simplicity. Each of us will find some sort of balance in our own way, but laughter is a quick way to see life in a lighthearted manner. It helps to take out the perpetual sting of the seriousness of our constant accountable actions. Several years ago I attended a workshop on the inner child. We were asked to visualize ourselves as a happy-go-lucky child. I was amazed that so few people could come up with a memory, or a picture in their minds, of a playful, fun-loving child.

Sometimes that little inner child in us all just wants to play! A little child who doesn't need judgment, expectations, competition, or criticism. It's the child that loves to watch ants, look at the stars, or wade through a puddle. That child is in all of us, all of the time. Some people have an overactive child and appear to be flighty, irresponsible, and immature. Some people have an over-protective or critical parent overriding the child. They follow all the rules, play life safe, and seldom find real joy in everyday life. They do what they're told to do. They believe what they're taught to believe.

We need the 'adult' mediator between the two. There is a balance between being spontaneous and free and being responsible and self-accountable. Each person is very different in finding their own line—but there is a line. Our 'inner child' is based on what you were like as a young child, wanting to be free of time, commitments, people, or places. It's the part of you that is silly and humorous, a jokester, or a magician. It's the child you can visualize on a swing, jungle gyms, playing with a puppy or hitting/catching a ball. The inner child has those moments of awe, wonder, curiosity, and play. As adults we wish, in those moments, that they'd continue forever. It's the secret we keep to ourselves because it's just not very 'grown-up' and we're afraid what others will think about our maturity level. So we become stoic adults—no room for the child within us. Stuff it down—letting it come up only once in a great while. But after that workshop, I decided that it was important to keep my inner child alive and happy. So at least once a day, I visualize little blond me doing twirls on the mountain top and laughing with joy. She helps me to feel that joy, even if it's for only a moment. That feeling, that visualization, helps the adult in me to relax and reprioritize. She reminds me that joy and laughter are important. If I haven't laughed that day, I seek it out. I'll go to a playground, call or see someone that makes me laugh, or I read jokes or watch a funny movie, and animal antics always make me laugh. They say laughter is the best medicine. It's true—but only if you truly feel it. Your head can't create that joy or passion, only your heartfelt emotions can.

I hope you can come up with a visualization or a photo of you as a young person laughing, enjoying, and feeling good about life. Hold it in your thoughts, see as many details as you can, then feel what he/she feels at that moment. Practice if you need to. Then when you've had a hard day, see the young you and feel the simplicity. Maybe in those few moments, you'll slightly adjust your priorities, smile a bit, or just feel a little lighter. Our bodies, brains, and hearts need a break sometimes from the chaos of everyday life. So find a way to laugh, feel light hearted, or just savor a moment of pure wonderment and joy.

Be the Babbling Brook
Let the joyful child in you bubble up to the surface and play.

INSIGHTS TO PONDER

1. Take the time to visualize a healthy, happy, fun-loving you as a youngster. Hold on to that picture in your mind:
   - See if you can feel what he/she is feeling.
   - Name it—what was the feeling?
   - Can you recall a time in the last week that felt like that?
   - Why or why not? Explain your answer

2. When was the last time you belly laughed?
   - How did that feel?
   - Who were you with or what was the situation, or where were you?
   - Is there a place or a person who makes you laugh the most?

3. If you were the manager of you (which you are)—what would you require in order to stay healthy and happy?

4. If you were the president or CEO of a company, would you require your employees to take time and have some fun? Laugh? Play? What would the benefits be? Downfall? Do you know any companies that are currently doing this?

5. How do you balance the inner child with the adult?
   - What actions do you consider too childish?
   - How has your critical adult kept you too safe, too responsible, too mature?
   - What could you try today/tomorrow in order to have a joyful, laughable, or playful moment in your day?

6. Why do you need to be more lighthearted and playful?

7. What would people say if you did something playful? What would you tell yourself? How could you create these moments (so others don't notice, if you're in a place where you can't show it) but you get the joy?

8. A babbling brook reminds me to be lighthearted and playful—what reminds you to be lighthearted and playful? Is it strong enough to get your attention? Do you take action?

9. Practice playful adventure inside and/or outside of yourself (both forms work).

NOTES

A WISH FOR ME

To hear music
    but sing my own songs
To see color
    but sense the necessity of black and white
To be a part of something
    Yet, apart from it.

To see and hear alike
    yet different
To be a part of others
    yet distinctly me.

To feel as only I can feel
To sing as only I can sing
To be what only I can be
To myself—Not others.

Yes, these are the things
    I wish for me.

CHAPTER 8

SO MANY PATHS

WATERWAYS: SO MANY PATHS

Not long ago I was on a vacation with my husband, going north on the Mississippi River between Wisconsin and Iowa. There on the boat, I noticed a lot of little islands and off-chutes or inlets from the main river. We had to maneuver around the low level of water, the islands, and the dead-end inlets. It made me think of how we human beings all start out the same at birth, but from that moment on our lives take off on different paths until we reach the end (the waters end—the ocean) of our lives through death.

I have always been amazed at how each person's life has a story unique to itself. It is just like the river—unpredictable, playing out its unique opportunities, and adjusting or changing when necessary. Like those waterways, some people seem to be on only one path, while others may have reasons to juke around the islands or explore an inlet. Those in the inlets may find other waterway connections and some may find a dead-end having to return to the main river. All the different ways create curiosity, exploration, and adventure. Think for a moment—where would you be without curiosity, courage, and/or an adventurer's spirit? It brings life to our habits, routines, and the everyday momentum.

Sometimes the paths are in our plans, and sometimes it's just a spontaneous challenge. No matter how you flow down the river, it's your own way, and it's very personal. It is a journey to be honored no matter how it was derived. It's a journey only you could have taken and experienced no matter how many others have crisscrossed the waterways before or after you. It saddens me to see how few people truly honor their journey. It's not about the competition of whose life is better or worse. It is *your* journey! Nobody experienced it like you did. Embrace your path. It's truly unique to you. Sometimes we get so caught up with what others are doing that we forget about our own uniqueness.

We are taught to compare our path to others. Then we judge it, change our expectations to accommodate what others think we should be doing, or we fret and worry about doing it right. All the while knowing that no one else will see it, think it, or feel it like we do as individuals. So why do we compare the journeys? Because we're human social beings and competition is a way for us to feel alive. So we listen to what others have to say. Whether we feel strong or insecure in some way, their words will influence our paths. If you feel committed or passionate about your current path, you'll stay the course and become even stronger to see your course through to the end. If you feel like you're generally on the right path but may need to tweak it a bit, someone's opinion may influence you to seek out new information and maybe try something in addition to what you're already doing. If you're really insecure about who you are, what you want, or where you're going you'll let others' ideas take you down their path, whether it's good for you or not. That's not to say that any of these choices are a bad thing. It's up to you to be influenced or not. Sometimes the new journey creates a new passion, sometimes it empowers or encourages you, or it can entrench you. You're at the helm—the choices are yours. But even though we have a need to be an individual on our own unique path, we have a need to be connected to others in one form or another. It's really more about how much you let others influence you.

Waterways also teach us about the importance of staying connected—how to stay together. No matter how many tributaries there are, they all feed into a main source—the river, stream, lake, or ocean. Without water, neither our bodies nor this planet would survive as we know it. Connection is like a large river. It is like our family, or the human race. Or maybe it's a tributary, like a culture, a religion, or a profession that feeds into the larger river. We all have dreams, desires, needs, and wants. We get to choose how much connection we want—but we all need some. That connection may be to nature, animals, and or human beings. But we all have to find our source to keep us connected to this planet.

The waterways show us that while we're busy on our own unique journeys, we still belong to the planet. You belong to the river called the human race. We need our connections as much as we need our uniqueness. Find your stability—go and find your people, your animal to love, or your place in nature to walk—get connected, then go explore!

Be the Waterways
Connected yet Unique

INSIGHTS TO PONDER

1. Sit back and think about "your personal journey."
   - Were you determined to be someone or become a characteristic (kind, outgoing, generous . . .), a profession, a parent, etc.?
   - Why did you choose that particular focus?
   - Have others' words influenced you? How?
   - Have others' words influenced you more often to the negative or positive direction? What state of mind/ heart were you in when you made those changes?
   - From 1 (low) to 10 (high), how would you rate your life so far with regard to your strong decisions?
   - How have you honored your decisions?

2. Have you ever started a path and decided it wasn't really what you wanted?
   - How did you feel?
   - Were others trying to convince you to stay the course?
   - Did you feel strong, weak, or ready for some new information?
   - How did your internal feeling about yourself influence your decisions?
   - What influences could have changed your path and why do you believe that?

3. What keeps you connected? What keeps you grounded when life gets stressful?

4. Who or what do you honor that helped keep you on the journey? What are you most proud of?

5. Who or what do you hold responsible or honor for making your journey difficult/easy?

6. How do you see yourself as a unique person upon this planet?

7. In the future, what would it look like to be connected and content in life? What is your balance of uniqueness vs connection?

NOTES

BECOMING ME

I look at where I started
    I'm amazed at how I've grown
I'm grateful for the lessons
    Of things I'd never known.

I look back at who I've become
    I wonder why I chose
To be me, in this way
    While many paths arose.

I look back and I marvel
    At choices that I've weighed
I'm glad that I have chosen
    To love this life I've made.

Photo Location: Yellowstone River, Yellowstone Nat'l Park, Wyoming

CHAPTER 9

EXPANSION OF ONESELF

THE RIVER'S PROGRESSION

The fascinating thing about rivers and streams is that, in general, they keep joining up with other kinds of bodies of water like a larger river, or a lake until they drop into an ocean or sea. Our human lives are very much in sync with the same process. We were born, raised in a family, made friends, and marry/partner into other families. We go from being an individual to knowing hundreds, thousands or millions by the time we die. As a thinker—a new thought comes to mind, then is shared, it's expounded upon, and split up and researched by individual parts then adding a new segment to the once single idea. As an emotion, let's say we meet someone new and you get a positive feeling about them. You two talk (feeling even more positive), and now you want more people to be part of this great feeling and you share it with others. So it doesn't matter if it's the river's story, a human being's story, a new thought or emotion's story—the process is the same from beginning to end.

Our lives are about expansion from the day we're born until the day we die. We learn new concepts, meet new people, explore new cultures, feel new feelings, think new thoughts and develop a life that we're (hopefully) proud of. We're constantly growing larger just like the streams that connect to a river which in turn connects to the lake or ocean. You have become the ocean. Think about all you've learned since the day you were born. You have grown into an amazing human being. You have five senses that are constantly teaching you about new things. Think about all that you've touched, tasted, smelled, heard, or seen. Now, on top of that, add in biology, communications, personality, etc. Now aren't you a spectacular growing being? I'm thinking that some major honoring of yourself should be going on here. Remember that you, too, are a part of a process of growing and expanding. Perhaps you've added new skills, discovered new talents, or been challenged by a new idea. Your nature is to be more than you currently are in every minute of every day. Embrace your true nature. Don't minimize yourself or your abilities—be genuinely proud of who you are and what you're creating. The world needs more people to shine. In shining we allow others to shine, too. Maybe one day we'll have a lot more people shining, believing in their worth and expansion. So when you see two rivers converging, take the time to do a little introspection of the *you* that just keeps expanding, too.

Be the streams, rivers, lakes, and oceans
Expand—merging and growing to become an incredible
YOU!

INSIGHTS TO PONDER

1. Think back to this past week. List ten new things that you've learned.

2. What are your favorite areas to learn about? Are there any themes/areas do you dislike?

3. How has your life expanded to where you are now? Were there any expansions that you liked or were helpful to you?

4. What about the expansions in your life that created chaos, discontent, or resentment? How did they help you expand?

5. What ways have you merged/expanded?
   - Marriage/partnership/relationship
   - School/Job
   - Activities/social/clubs
   - Physical ailments
   - Having children
   - Having pets
   - A religion/spiritual belief
   - Cultural/History/Heritage
   - Others?

6. Have you changed your process over the years? What works now?

7. How do you take care of you and your expansiveness? Have you figured out your balance?

8. If you could grow/expand in the future, where or what would that look like?

CLARITY OF LIMITATIONS

The skies know no limitations
My potential lies therein
Will I reach my destination?
Or there—will I just begin?

Sometimes I feel like I've given it all
When's enough—enough?
If nature is my leader
Must the journey be so rough?

My limitations are within me
As I look to the sky to give
Is this just self-imposed?
Or just beginning to live?

I am?

CHAPTER 10

CLARITY AND INTEGRITY

SEEING THROUGH THE WATER

Have you ever seen a body of water that you can see through? It's so clear that it looks like a window to the rock bed below. It's spectacular to see the fish, plants, rocks, and debris. When I can see clearly into the water I don't question what's beneath me—I know where everything is. If the body of water is murky then I get nervous because I can't tell what's really going on beneath me. Is it sandy or muddy where I could get stuck? Are there slick rocks to tumble over? Will fish nibble at my legs or a shark bite me when I'm in the shallow part of the ocean?

Our lives are very much like the clear or murky waters. So try this on: let's put your whole life on the front page of a national newspaper or the headliner on the internet. Would you worry about what people would think? Would you be afraid that you'd lose your friends, family members, or main relationship like a spouse, partner, boyfriend/girlfriend? Would you feel the urge to call your boss and explain? Could you live with your secrets being exposed? Would it hurt someone else? What would you feel? It wasn't about having others approval or not—it's about whether you feel guilt, shame, embarrassment, or self-loathing. Could I take the worst secret or mistake I'd made and live with it if everybody knew? What would I say to explain the scenario or issue? Who would stand with me, no matter what? Who would leave me?

I remember hearing the 'newspaper story as a way to live your life' philosophy back in my early college days, so I was maybe around 19 – 22 years old. I don't remember who said it or if I read it or where I got this information. But I've never forgotten it. It changed my life in how I thought about clarity of character and the actions we hold to. So before I did something questionable, I'd ask myself, "How would this look on the front page of the newspaper?" Could I live with the fall out? How would I justify it to myself, or others? How could the ripple effect hurt me in the future? Would others be hurt because of this decision? This doesn't mean that I didn't make some bad decisions because I did. But it did make me stop and pause for a moment to think it through. This was just another way to have a self-check about integrity. If I say one thing and do another, I've lost credibility. As I look back there are things that I have done that I still wouldn't change (though others did not approve of what I did). This is about self-accountability, self-responsibility, and self-respect. Everyone's idea of a concept or issue can be different. But this isn't about doing what others think you should do. This is about you. How do you feel about yourself, your past, and what motivates you? Be clear to yourself—know what you're willing to take a hit for or take a stand for. How would you defend, rationalize, or maybe apologize if need be? Remember the murky waters? The more you muddy your water, the more people won't believe you, trust in you, or stand by you.

If you have things in your past that you're hiding, then start dealing with them. Be selective of who you tell but stop shaming yourself. Take accountability for your past and current actions, whether positive or negative. We need to be responsible for ourselves! Blaming someone else is self-deception. Find your part in it (this does not include any form of abuse) and forgive yourself or promise to make it better in the future. Your negative energy toward yourself is using up the space for good energy to be utilized in the future. Figure out what you need to do to feel better about that situation. If there's no way to really 'clean it up' then, what do you need to tell yourself in-order to finally "let it go"? Know there are always people out there that have done less or more than you have when it comes to mistakes. All those mistakes made you who you are today. So if you don't like you, make better decisions. Don't keep mucking up the water. Hold yourself to a better standard. The good news is that we can learn, grow and create something better in the future. Integrity is all we have. If your words and actions aren't getting the good results that you want, then you need to do some self-analysis. Most likely others aren't seeing your integrity. Learn to be clear to yourself about who you are. What standards do you hold yourself to? What actions are showing others who you really are? Find your clarity—live in clarity.

Be the Water
Be Clear—Live in Integrity

INSIGHTS TO PONDER

1. List something in your past that holds you back because you don't want someone to know about it. Then ask the following questions:
   - Why am I afraid/ashamed/concerned?
   - Who would it affect?
   - What's the best scenario and worst scenario for an outcome if this information were shared?
   - How would it effect my future?

2. Taking that same scenario:
   - How does it feel right now when you think of it?
   - How is it holding you back?
   - How would you feel if that information were out?

3. Taking that same scenario list all the options to rid or neutralize that issue.

4. Now with that list add what you think the outcomes/ expectations would be for each option.

5. Choose one option and write down your first step. Could you set a time frame to complete that step? If so, do it!

6. Write down how it would feel if this was no longer an issue to you.

7. Write down: How does it feel for you to be in control of your life instead of the "issue" being in control of your life?

8. Repeat all these steps with any other issues that stop you from being the best you.

9. If your life were on the front page of a newspaper what would you be proud of? Make a list of all the good decisions you've made. Look at the list often to validate the great you that you've already created.

NOTES

MOMENTS OF INSIGHT

There was a time
    for laughter and play
Enjoying my family
    all part of a day.

There was a time
    for questions and talk
a deep conversation
    with friends I would walk.

There was a time
    for decisive thoughts
A beckoning silence
    my stomach in knots.

There is a time
    when all is right
when time is replaced
    with moments of insight.

Photo Location: Rocky Mountain Nat'l Park, Grand Lake, Colorado.

CHAPTER 11

REFLECTION

WATERS ARE REFLECTIVE

The reflection from the water on a clear calm day can be uncannily beautiful—an exact replica of nature herself. We, too, need to see our real self and not believe that the replica is real. Unlike Narcissus, the Greek God who fell in love with his own reflection, we need to find a way to reflect on our past and our current self. Who have we become? Do we like that person? Do we want to make changes that better suit our belief in ourselves? Reflective waters calm us down so we can take a look inside. The calmer the water the better the reflection. Reflection isn't about loving what's not real, like Narcissus. It's about learning to love the person you created deep inside. It may be the *you* that others don't see as often. It may be the *you* whose roots are deep and you work at letting yourself show outwardly more often. Regardless, it's the opportunity to see yourself for who you really are. Reflection is about being calm enough to be open to self-exploration. The more we understand about our beliefs and personality characteristics the better we can guide ourselves toward meaningful fulfillment.

Reflection will not look the same to each person. It's meant to be a situation both outside and inside of you that gives you the space to let go. The fewer restraints you place on yourself and your environment for this exploration, the easier it'll be to do it. So try not to have a time constraint, or only this particular chair to sit in, or only when certain flowers are blooming (just kidding!). Why? Because reflection can be sitting in a parking lot searching why a meeting just went side-ways, or taking a walk, or finding meaning to a dream before you get out of bed, or contemplating about yourself after reading an article. All reflection is important and necessary in order to challenge yourself. Some people find self-reflection through meditation, prayer, silenced get-a-ways, or communion in nature. All these are wonderful ways to set the mood and open the heart and mind for true reflection. Allow yourself opportunities to arise that can be helpful to your in-depth practice.

A key theme here is quiet, calm, and alone. Some people are very fearful of alone time. They don't know what to do with their thoughts; they're afraid to look inside. Maybe they won't like what they see. Or maybe they've been taught that it's non-productive. Maybe they just can't find the time. There are many reasons we don't want to take the time or effort to reflect. I challenge you to do this. It is a way to combine our ability of both mind and heart. It syncs them up. If you aren't spending any alone time to synch up, then you probably don't know yourself very well. Your heart and mind are like neighbors instead of immediate family living together. When the heart and mind work together they can answer questions, problem-solve, or find new creative solutions.

I find in today's world that there is so much noise. It's the environmental noises, or the internal self-talk of chaos-making, or technology in its constant dinging, that makes it so much harder to quiet oneself. If you believe that being an authentic person is important, then it'll be worth the extra effort to find time for your self-reflection. Do you currently set aside time to allow your thoughts and feelings a chance to commune? In these chaotic times it's more important than ever to know yourself, what you believe in, who you trust, what passions are developing, and how you feel fulfilled. This is self-survival.

So how do you move yourself from shallow questioning into the deeper challenging questions? First of all, the way you'll learn to question yourself is to always ask about yourself. Don't let the ego change your course of thought. Ego wants to take you away from yourself and find the chaos in your world or others, not you. Stay the course. Here's an example: "My friend Jake isn't being a good friend. What makes a good friend? Am I a good friend? Who am I a good friend to, and how is it different from my friendship with Jake? What kind of friend am I to Jake? Would I need to change something to be a better friend? What are my beliefs about friendship? How do I show my beliefs? If I were a better friend would he respond differently? If he didn't respond positively, what would I want to do about our friendship? What matters to me the most about my friendship with Jake? Can this friendship allow me to show my beliefs and keep myself in synch with authenticity?"

Can you feel the depth of these questions? Can you see why it's important to question your beliefs, your thoughts, feelings and actions? We don't question everything we do—but we should question everything that is causing pain, heartache, or disillusionment within ourselves. Don't let the ego beat you up. Find what you believe, and then stick to it (until it's not valid any more). If what you come up with is freeing, solving a problem, or making you feel stronger, then you're on the right course.

Reflecting on your life helps you to honor it, and to help you prepare for your future of fulfillment. Let it help you create a space so that you can lovingly pat yourself on the back. Find your focus, understand your own perceptions, and find appreciation and gratitude toward yourself and others. We have to learn that to get what we want we need to believe it first.

So if you want a good relationship, then you have to be that good person that others want to be in a relationship with. You have to discover what you really believe about yourself. If you say, "I deserve a good partner" but your belief system says, "I'm not worthy of a good partner," the belief system will always be the attracting force. Your subconscious beliefs will always override whatever you say to yourself and others. Affirmations only work if you *truly* believe them. Beliefs guide the energy of what will be attracted to us. Self-reflection is a way to discover and connect to that deeper side of ourselves. Don't let the surface reflection fool you into believing something about yourself that is inaccurate or untrue. Look into the reflection of the water. Look into your depth and find the parts that you truly believe in. Then become more and more of that authentic you. Don't be like Narcissus, and fall in love with your reflection of who you think you might be. Be in love with who you really are. Go deep!

Be the Reflective Water
Know who you really are!

INSIGHTS TO PONDER

1. Have you taken time recently to contemplate or reflect upon you, your life, or your future? How did it feel?

2. Make a list of what stops you from finding reflective time.

3. What would be the benefit or consequence of finding reflective time?

4. Does one outweigh the other? Why?

5. What areas in your life do you feel are difficult? List them.

6. Now looking at that list, take the first one (do this with each one on the list):
   - Ask yourself one deeper question about it.
   - Do three more questions.
   - Finally, ask yourself what is your belief about it: "What do I believe_____ should be? Why?"
   - Why do you believe what you believe?
   - Who is it beneficial to? (you and/or others)

7. Write down times and places throughout your day that you could ask yourself one to five deeper questions? (remember you need to be quiet, calm and alone). If not, what's stopping you?

8. Do you believe you are capable of deeper reflection? Is it important to you?

9. Contemplate! Reflect! Challenge yourself.

BAD DAYS GONE

I know I have
Bad days
Sometimes
On that I can't deny.

Hurting others
Just isn't
Me
I can't help wonder why.

I want to smile
Like others
Do
I know my heart will sigh.

I will be free
Smiling with
Ease
I know my soul will fly.

Kindness toward others
A rippling
Effect
A joy one can't buy.

Photo Location: Clement Park, Littleton, Colorado

CHAPTER 12

RIPPLE EFFECT

YOUR RIPPLE EFFECT

Did you ever stand at the edge of a pond/lake and throw or skip stones into it, just to watch the ripple it made? As a child, I could spend hours doing just that. I loved to watch how big and how far away the ripples would go from where the stone landed. The heavier the stone, the greater the impact. Human energy works in a similar way. The greater the emotional intent, the greater the impact. My *thoughts* will attract like energies to me. If I *believe* strongly about something it will come faster to me. So thinking about something sets a path for energy to follow but it is the emotions/beliefs that will bring it quicker or slower. If I'm ho-hum about it, that neutrality creates confusion. The energy says, "so which way do you want me to go?" Hence, no movement is felt in either direction.

The ripple effect is created in a direction. It will go to the positive or negative. Just like the ripple effect from a stone being thrown into the water, our energy puts out energy ripples or waves. Other people and objects around you will feel your energy whether you want them to or not. Everything on this planet is energy based. So energy will react to the wave effects of others. Energy draws or attracts like energy: positive to positive or negative to negative. Here's an example: you get up "on the wrong side of the bed," it seems like every little thing that could go wrong does, all day long. You may stub your toe, get caught in traffic, or hear a snippy comment. If you change that energy, positive to positive, your day just seems to go better. My mom would always say that when you're having a rough day, put a smile on your face, wear your favorite clothing, fix your hair, and take on the day. What I like to say is, "Fake it 'til you make it!" It just seemed to go better because I felt better about me.

When we feel good about who we are, then we see things differently. When we believe that we don't deserve to feel good difficult people and situations are then drawn to us. My energy will subconsciously seek out other matching negative energies and the negative effect just keeps playing out. Remember that *anything* negative or positive can come back to you. Similar or 'like' energies can come from anywhere, not just the 'people' category. So a bug flies into my eye, I hit every red light, my favorite salad is sold out. See how this is working?

This concept is hard to understand because other things are playing out at the same time. So positive people don't always get good things and negative people don't always get bad things happening to them. This is a general happening which is small compared to the big events which were set in place before the Laws of Attraction were to play out. When the big stuff is set in place it's for our soul's growth. After all, some of our best growth comes from difficulty. If a positive person never had difficulty they would never learn what they're capable of becoming or the depth of feeling they could experience. So while we don't get to choose the event that is happening to us or choose to have only positive events occur, we do get to choose our own reaction to the event.

One of the highest forms of moving energy is through belief. Remember that the belief will outweigh the words. That's why you can say affirmations until you're blue in the face and things may not change. It's more about how much do you truly believe what you're saying? Once the subconscious becomes conscious we can now knowingly choose energy to be in one place or another. We can even heal through energy work with great modalities like Healing Touch and Reiki. If you can understand this concept, you'll soon realize how powerful energy really is. How powerful you really are!

What I find fascinating is *collective energy*. This is about a group of people feeling the same way. In their concentration they can work energy to help a single person, a group of people or effect the energy around the world. For example, parents often worry about the safety of their deployed military sons and daughters who are far away on a mission. These parents sit back helplessly wondering what they can do. My response is to send heartfelt wishes/prayers for safety, then visualize them in a safe way. Ask family and friends to do the same. It is much better for everyone if that positive energy goes out rather than the negative energy of worrying. We should never under-estimate what like energies can do as a mass. Like energies from all over the world are busy attracting and adding more and more like energies. Mothers of children from every war torn nation, friends, family, spouses and partners, all wanting peace and safety. We have an ability to genuinely change for the good, through the belief that we can live in peace. The sad thing is that it can happen in the negative, too. Fear creeped into the USA within one year when one tragedy after another happened. We had the Columbine High School shooting, Oklahoma Federal Building bombing, and on 9/11, the Trade

Center and Pentagon tragedy. The fear that we weren't safe overcame all other forms of our American lifestyles. Our safe America was rocked. Our fear soaring out of control has not yet subsided. More and more tragedies in schools, theaters, churches, nightclubs, and malls are occurring. No longer can we go to places where there was once a feeling of guaranteed safety.

Not any one person is responsible for our negative attracting energies. But collective energy is. Our ripple effect of fear is felt throughout the world. While fear is strong, remember we live in the world of opposites. Have you noticed how many people are taking a stand for the good? Issues that have long been under the table are being brought to light. Thousands stand for the good of all people and millions more send loving wishes into the collective energy. I, for one, am excited about the movements to benefit all people—gender equality, LGBTQ, diversity, religious freedom, and acceptance. Remember that everything is perception, so the more you want to see the good, the more you will! We are given countless opportunities to practice finding the good. We do get to choose our reactions to events and people, even the difficult ones. I'll never forget, as a counselor in a high school next door to Columbine High School, the outpouring of love and care from all over the world. Though our shock and sadness felt overwhelming, it unified the world in compassion. What an incredible gift to the whole planet. I am not minimizing the hurt, but I am maximizing the choice of moving forward rather than staying stuck in fear. The choices we make every day help determine our quality of life. For example, we know that positive people heal faster, live longer, and are happier in general. Research has proven this to be true. So the question is, "what are you choosing to see?" What is your ripple effect? Can you tell what kind of things are coming back to you? Are you saying one thing and believing another? You may want to pay attention for greater insight and clarity. We're accountable for what we put out there through our own energy. Are you making your corner brighter or darker?

People are afraid, but it would benefit ourselves and others if we at least neutralized the fear-based living. You may want to say, "It is what it is—many things are out of my control." Because, in truth, how much control do you have over most situations? You can educate and inform. You can't make others comply with your beliefs, it's up to them to make that decision. You get to decide what's important to you and how you want to handle it. "It is what it is," is not about throwing your arms up in the air and doing nothing—it is about putting it in perspective of what you can do. "I can't solve all the problems of the world, but I can do this_____." It's taking the massive problem and making it into something that you can do like "I could send money" or "I can send positive prayers (wishes)" or "I'm going to volunteer at the food bank today, so I can help out in some way." It's in our nature to want to do something when difficulty around us is happening. Most of us get stuck on doing nothing because we become overwhelmed with *what* to do. Just do something—even if it's just sending wishes/prayers. To do nothing doesn't make us feel any better. But by consciously doing something, *anything*, we will feel better. It'll help us to see the good in the world, and maybe even help create a better world.

Keeping that in mind—"What is your ripple effect?" Do you understand just how powerful you are? You are affecting everything on this planet either consciously, subconsciously, or collectively. How do you want to affect this planet? Negative ripple effects can be just as powerful as the positive ones. So be careful in what you choose to believe, say, do, and be. Let your ripple effect represent who you really are—regardless of what you believe about energy. Your ripple effect will have impact. Your smile can make someone's day, who then makes someone else's day. Or maybe your anger demeans a person who then hurts someone else. Your choice.

In the grand scheme of things, my hope is that as you age and review your life, you will feel good. Your review will let you feel all the love and joy you created, as well as the hurt and sorrow you created while you were on this planet. The fact is you'll never know how many ripples you created in a single action. It'll affect many over your lifetime. Choose and practice being a positive ripple effect.

As the rain drop affects the pond,
so does your energy affect everything on our planet earth.
Be a positive ripple effect.

INSIGHTS TO PONDER

1. Looking back at your past—can you find a time when your actions created more reactions from others? How did that feel? Were you proud or ashamed?

2. What decisions did you make about your personality traits once you understood the ripple effect?

3. How have you seen the "ripple effect" in social media? Have you been a part of it and how did you feel? Are there limits that you've placed on yourself within social media? Has that been helpful or too limiting?

4. List the ways you are consciously influencing your ripple effect on others?

5. Rating it from 1-100, how often do you believe that you create a positive ripple effect? What future number would you like to attain?

6. If you asked five friends about your ripple effect, what would they say about how you affect them? (actually, do ask them, if you're comfortable with it).

7. Watch the movie, "Pay it Forward," by Peter Abrams

8. List one negatively impactful thing you do (we all have many!) that you'd like to change. List one positive thing you do that you'd like to do more of.

9. Make a pact with yourself to decrease the negative and increase your positive ripple effect. Pay attention to how it makes you feel.

I AM

I am the one
who controls
that which I am.

I am the one
who feels
the stains of I.

I am the one
who knows
who feels
who needs
Or complies.

I am the one
which is
"I."

CHAPTER 13

THE POWER OF THE WATERFALL

THE POWERFUL WATERFALL

When we look at life and the waterfall we notice how much they look the same. When we're in a season of drought the water trickles over the falls. In a season of rain, the swollen river creates an astonishing display of water cascading down the falls with a force like none other. Our lives run parallel to nature's drought/abundance. For example: we may have days, months, or years, where life is hard and we feel drained— nothing left to give. We throw our arms up in the air and yell, "Really? Seriously, I can't take much more!!" We all get those times when we're down and out, depressed, confused, hurt, or disillusioned. The days drag on and our hope is that it'll end soon, much like the dried up river and trickling waterfall. Yet in our heart of hearts, we know that the rains will once again come and replenish both our lives and the life of the river.

I know that those times are real and necessary in order to grow, re-establish oneself, or try to find rhyme and reason for one's life. I also know that the rains do come and can change an outcome in a matter of seconds. Have you watched the news and seen a wall of water whisking away homes, businesses, and cars? That little creek or river became an unstoppable power to be dealt with. It's not taking a back seat, it lets us know who's in charge in that moment. Have you ever felt that feeling of being unstoppable? Your adrenaline is ponding, excitement is all around, like no person or thing is going to stop you. You can feel the powerful energy surging through your veins. You walk out to do your presentation and you nail it. You talk to your spouse about a pressing matter and know you got the message across. You interview for a job, and know you nailed it. There are scenarios after scenarios with moments in time when everything came together and we got what we wanted or needed. We hopped onto the adventure ride and can feel the excitement of the journey. But just as floods don't happen every day neither do we get many energy surges and that's probably a good thing. If you think back to those times it took a lot of energy to stay at the top like that. I don't know about you but I find it hard to stay in that state for very long. I'm exhausted when it's all over.

Though we experience too little or too much occasionally, most of us spend most of our time in the normal everyday levels. It goes up or down a little but not enough to cause a drain or anxiety. Our little ups and downs may feel more like contentment or a little stressed out. But it's not enough to hurt us one way or another. It's actually a lot easier on us to be in the normal energy ranges than in the extremes—positively or negatively. Do you ever feel odd because your life just feels 'normal'? Everybody's normal is different. What one can tolerate, someone else can't. What is relaxing simplicity to one is boring to another—that's what makes us all unique. Some people love the action of the adrenaline flowing lifestyle while others sit at home cooking and watching TV. No one is wrong or right, it's all preference. The amount of energy your body has will help determine what kind of lifestyle suits you. The turtle will move slower than the energized bunny. But both will succeed in their own way. I'm sure we all know people who can only accomplish one task at a time. They may not have much energy in general, so they need to focus on the task at hand. They are methodical and persevering. We also know people who do circles around others and are just as content and happy. Both accomplish what's necessary, both have different ways to do it, and both are comfortable in their personal natures. Just like the river has a normal level of flowing, so do we.

Most of us like to be at the top of our normal to feel good about who we are, what we stand for, and what we're capable of giving back. We can sustain ourselves for some time at this level—it feels good, feels successful, and we are not drained or diminished. We feel good about our power and how to balance it, in between the normal low and the normal high. The normal range in our lives helps us to know stability. We need the extremes to grow, to change, to push us in a direction we've not known or understood before. It tests our boundaries, our beliefs, our commitments. We learn how much more we can become. Just like the swollen river drives a waterfall to plunge hundreds of feet, carving out and redirecting the river's path. When it's time for a change, change will happen—often without your permission or your conscious awareness. Much like a flash flood, we, too, will often not expect the change. That's the beauty of nature. That is also the beauty of who we are and who we are challenged to become.

It's okay to be content, just like the normal flow of the waterfall. It's where we are most of the time—normal is good! Then when the surge of change comes, just like the overflowing waterfall, give it all you've got. Maximize yourself and be that powerful waterfall—unique, unpredictable and fierce.

*Like the Waterfall: Understand your Flow
Understand your Power.*

INSIGHTS TO PONDER

1. Looking at yourself, in general, how often (in percentages) is your energy:
   - _____ too low (dried up or barely flowing)
   - _____ normal (occasional ups and downs)
   - _____ too high (swollen river or a wall of water)

2. Can you look back at your life and see times of drought? List two or three, then answer these questions for each:
   - Was there a reason for your difficult time/drought?
   - How did you get through it?
   - How much energy did it take away from everyday living?
   - Looking back now, did it push you toward change?
   - Are you different today because of it?

3. When you get that surge of power, how do you use it?

4. What routinely makes you feel powerful?

5. Is that power beneficial to you *and* others?

6. Looking at your personality and lifestyle, are you more the turtle or the rabbit?
   - Do you like it? Or do you wish you were more like the other one?
   - Do you beat yourself up over it?
   - How have you accepted your style?
   - Is there anything you could do to like your lifestyle more?

7. In the future, would you like to possess more personal power?
   - Why?
   - What motivates your powerfulness?
   - How would you make it more beneficial to you and others?

NOTES

THEREFORE, I AM

I am who I am
I am powerful
I have choice
Therefore, I am

I am who I am
I am peaceful
I choose calm
Therefore, I am

I am who I am
I am gracious
I choose love
Therefore, I am

I am who I am
I am integrity
I do what I say
Therefore, I am

I am whatever I
Believe I am
So I choose
To be me
Therefore, I AM

ABOUT THE AUTHOR

Cheri Henke Kretsch grew up as a mountain girl in Colorado. Born as a carefree lover of life, the only world she knew was filled with animals, nature and a loving family. After experiencing traumatic events in childhood and adolescence, the mountains taught her, once again, to trust and love. Living in nature gave her the eyes to see healing, the strength to go on and the heart to share. Her love of nature and the metaphors it creates became a life-long gift to help understand the world she lives in.

Cheri Henke Kretsch is a licensed psychotherapist with twenty-seven years of experience working for large companies, on military bases, and in private practice. In addition, Henke Kretsch has spent over twenty years teaching psychology, working with special-needs students, working as a guidance counselor at the high school level, and working as an adjunct professor of psychology at the college level.

Henke Kretsch is the recipient of the Outstanding Young Educator Award for Kansas and was twice awarded Who's Who in Education. She was Counselor of the Year for Jefferson County Schools, Colorado, and won both the Golden and Silver Poets Award in Washington, DC. Cheri Henke Kretsch currently resides in Littleton, Colorado. She can be contacted at her email address: cheri@natural-lessons.com.